CREDIT TO
20th CENTURY-FOX
WILL BE APPRECIATED.

TWENTIETH CENTURY FOX

INSIDE THE PHOTO ARCHIVE

PREFACE BY TOM ROTHMAN & JIM GIANOPULOS

FOREWORD BY MARTIN SCORSESE

PHOTOGRAPHS SELECTED BY
ROB EASTERLA, KEVIN MURPHY, AND MILES SCOTT

HARRY N. ABRAMS, INC., PUBLISHERS

PROJECT MANAGER: Eric Himmel
EDITOR: Deborah Aaronson
BOOK AND JACKET DESIGN: Abbott Miller
with Johnschen Kudos, Pentagram
PRODUCTION MANAGER: Justine Keefe

Library of Congress Cataloging-in-Publication Data
Twentieth Century Fox : inside the photo archive / preface
by Tom Rothman and Jim Gianopulos ; foreword by Martin
Scorsese ; photographs selected by Rob Easterla, Kevin
Murphy, and Miles Scott.
    p. cm.
Includes bibliographical references and index.
ISBN 0-8109-4977-6
1. Documentary photography—United States. 2. Twentieth
Century-Fox Film Corporation—History. I. Easterla, Rob. II.
Murphy, Kevin. III. Scott, Miles. IV. Twentieth Century-Fox
Film Corporation.
  TR820.5.T84 2004
  779'.979143—dc22   2004011194

Printed and bound in China

10 9 8 7 6 5 4 3 2 1

 Harry N. Abrams, Inc.
100 Fifth Avenue
New York, N.Y. 10011
www.abramsbooks.com

Abrams is a subsidiary of

LA MARTINIÈRE
GROUPE

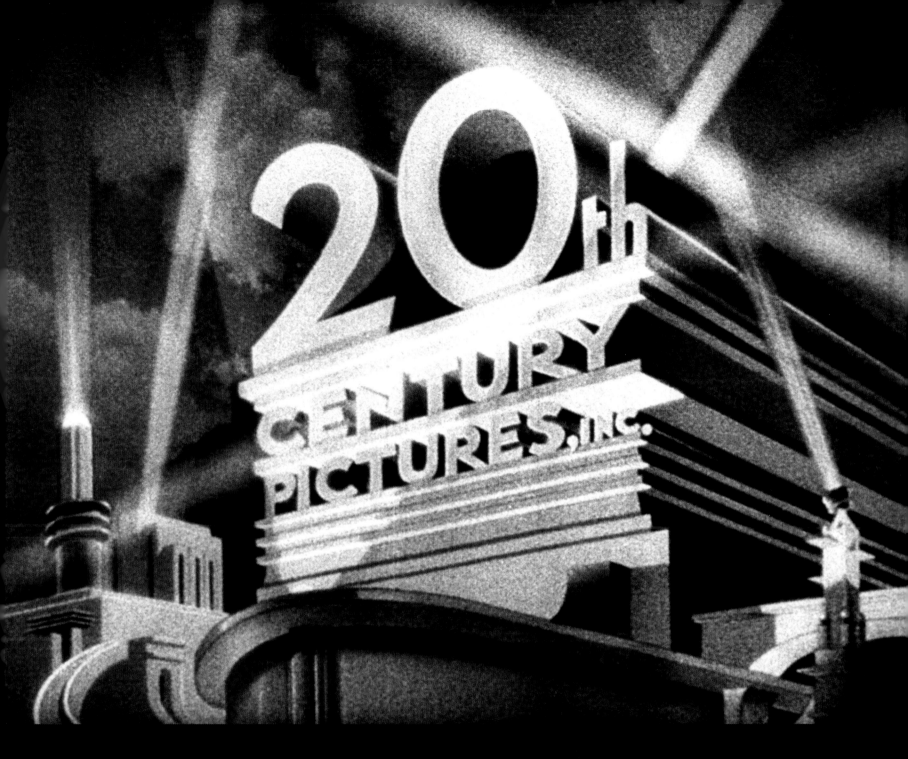

PREFACE

TOM ROTHMAN & JIM GIANOPULOS
CHAIRMEN, FOX FILM ENTERTAINMENT

There is one thing that sets a Major Motion Picture Studio apart from all other contemporary film enterprises: history. A true movie history cannot be purchased or licensed or created anew, not for all the technological revolution in the universe. It must have been "lived," or in the case of most studios, including our own, survived, and then preserved. All of us who have the privilege to work at Twentieth Century Fox are, for a time, custodians of an incomparable, irreplaceable, cultural history and we consider its stewardship one of our foremost obligations . . . and pleasures. Accordingly, we are greatly proud of the Twentieth Century Fox Photo Archive, which preserves the still record of our moving picture heritage.

The Fox Photo Archive maintains the still photography of Twentieth Century Fox and its pre-merger companies — Fox Film Corporation and Twentieth Century Pictures — in a state-of-the-art temperature/humidity-controlled storage on our historic Pico Boulevard Lot in Los Angeles. In addition to an ongoing conservation effort, archivists provide access to the ten-million-item collection for Fox entities and their licensees through collection management and development, instruction and referral based on knowledge of cinema history, photo editing, curatorial direction, research, and photo duplication. Collection holdings date from 1917 and include contemporary movie images that transfer to the Photo Archive seven years after a film's release date. A working collection that continues to grow through various accessions, the Photo Archive acquires an estimated 100,000 new images annually.

Within the pages of this book you will find a taste of those millions of images from dozens of gifted photographers. Some are from legendary films that have become cultural monuments, some from intriguing lesser-known movies in which a still nonetheless captured a unique enduring moment. All are arranged to showcase not so much the glory of the individual movies themselves as the rare art of freezing an instant of "moving history" and thus providing succinct visual insight into the defining art form of contemporary civilization. Plus, the shots are a gas, and the fun of looking at them, timeless. We hope you enjoy.

MOULIN ROUGE!, 2001
Nicole Kidman
Photographer: Ellen Von Unwerth

142

FOREWORD

MARTIN SCORSESE

Dream Factories. That's what people used to call the Hollywood studios — or maybe that's what the studios called themselves. At any rate, it's how they *wanted* to be known. The term stuck, and with good reason. The extraordinary artistry at every level of the studio hierarchy, from the actors to the sound recordists, from the directors to the gaffers, from the writers to the propmen, made for an atmosphere that was probably closer to a hellishly busy workshop than a production line. At a studio like Twentieth Century Fox, every single movie, from the A pictures to the least prestigious programmers, was the product of craftsmanship and artistry of the highest level. I often find myself hypnotized by lesser movies made during the heyday of the studio era, not to mention enduring classics like *How Green Was My Valley* or *All About Eve*. You really do feel that you are entering another world when you watch these pictures. The genius of the system, indeed.

What makes this book so special is the fact that it gives you not just the final results, the dreams themselves, but the process behind their creation. You see not only Shirley Temple and Peter Lorre in portraits of such exquisite black and white that the silver nitrate particles seem to scintillate before your eyes, but also Tyrone Power in costume relaxing on the set of *In Old Chicago*, the kitchen staff at the studio restaurant, a continuity man marking the set of *The Fly*, and Darryl Zanuck himself taking a moment to light his cigar on the set of *The Longest Day*. One of my favorite images is of Gene Tierney waiting to shoot the scene where she scatters her father's ashes on horseback in *Leave Her to Heaven* — if you study her face, you can see that her mood uncannily reflects the mood of the scene. Every photograph in this marvelous book speaks of a world now sadly gone by. Seen all together, they give you a sense of the dynamism, the excitement of people taking part in a grand new art form, *the* modern art form. Hollywood may not have been an easy place to work, but it always retained that sense of collective excitement.

In other words, this collection gives you not only the dreams, but, to quote Dashiell Hammett, the stuff that dreams are made of.

Alice Faye, c. 1935

PREVIOUS SPREAD

BUTCH CASSIDY AND
THE SUNDANCE KID, 1969
Paul Newman
Photographer: Jimmy Mitchell

WILD RIVER, 1960
Lee Remick

REMEMBER THE DAY, 1941
Claudette Colbert and John Payne

FOREVER AMBER, 1947
Glenn Langan

TARZAN'S REVENGE, 1938
Glenn Morris and Eleanor Holm

FOREVER AMBER, 1947
Richard Greene

MY DARLING CLEMENTINE, 1946
Victor Mature and Ward Bond

ARIZONA TO BROADWAY, 1933
James Dunn and Joan Bennett

ZORBA THE GREEK, 1964
Alan Bates and Anthony Quinn

21

THE SOUND OF MUSIC, 1965
Kym Karath and Jimmy Mitchell
Photographer: Jimmy Mitchell

THE ONLY GAME IN TOWN, 1970
Warren Beatty

WALKING DOWN BROADWAY, 1938
Jayne Regan, Leah Ray, and
Dixie Dunbar

LES MISÉRABLES, 1935
Rochelle Hudson (center)
Photographer: Bill Thomas

WILLIAM SHAKESPEARE'S
ROMEO + JULIET, 1996
Claire Danes
Photographer: Merrick Morton

MOULIN ROUGE!, 2001
Ewan McGregor
Photographer: Ellen Von Unwerth

26

FROM THE TERRACE, 1960
Paul Newman

HOW TO STEAL A MILLION, 1966
Peter O'Toole, William Wyler, and
Audrey Hepburn
Photographer: Terry O'Neill

NEXT STOP, GREENWICH
VILLAGE, 1976
Christopher Walken

LLOYD'S OF LONDON, 1936

IN OLD CHICAGO, 1938
Tyrone Power

THE OX-BOW INCIDENT, 1943
Henry Fonda

THE AGONY AND THE
ECSTASY, 1965
Rex Harrison

THE LONGEST DAY, 1962
Peter Lawford

THE BIG TRAIL, 1930
John Wayne
Photographer: Frank Powolny

THE INN OF SIXTH HAPPINESS, 1958
Ingrid Bergman

946-5-83

BUTCH CASSIDY AND
THE SUNDANCE KID, 1969
Paul Newman and Robert Redford

LOVE ME TENDER, 1956
Elvis Presley

THE GRAPES OF WRATH, 1940
Henry Fonda
Photographer: Emmett Schoenbaum

JULIA, 1977
Jane Fonda
Photographer: Eva Sereny

DRUMS ALONG THE
MOHAWK, 1939
Claudette Colbert and
Henry Fonda

PLENTY, 1985
Meryl Streep
Photographer: Frank Connor

TORA! TORA! TORA!, 1970   THE GHOST AND MRS. MUIR, 1947
                                 Gene Tierney
                                 Photographer: Jim Reid

ALL THAT JAZZ, 1979
Bob Fosse
Photographer: Josh Weiner

WHAT A WAY TO GO!, 1964
Shirley MacLaine

NORMA RAE, 1979
Sally Field

THE MARRIAGE-GO-ROUND, 1961
Julie Newmar

YOUNG FRANKENSTEIN, 1974
Cloris Leachman and Gene Wilder

THE KING OF COMEDY, 1983
Martin Scorsese and Robert De Niro

RAPTURE, 1965
Patricia Gozzi and Dean Stockwell

THE ONLY GAME IN TOWN, 1970
Elizabeth Taylor

PREVIOUS SPREAD

JOURNEY TO THE CENTER
OF THE EARTH, 1959
Arlene Dahl

JESSE JAMES, 1939
Tyrone Power
Photographer: Frank Powolny

MASTER AND COMMANDER:
THE FAR SIDE OF THE WORLD, 2003
Russell Crowe
Photographer: Stephen Vaughan

Shirley Temple, 1937
Photographer: Otto Dyar

LEAVE HER TO HEAVEN, 1945
Jeanne Crain

San-5-H28

BODY AND SOUL, 1931
Myrna Loy

Alice Faye, c. 1935

VALLEY OF THE DOLLS, 1967
Sharon Tate

THE KEYS OF THE KINGDOM, 1944
Gregory Peck

637-S-62

63

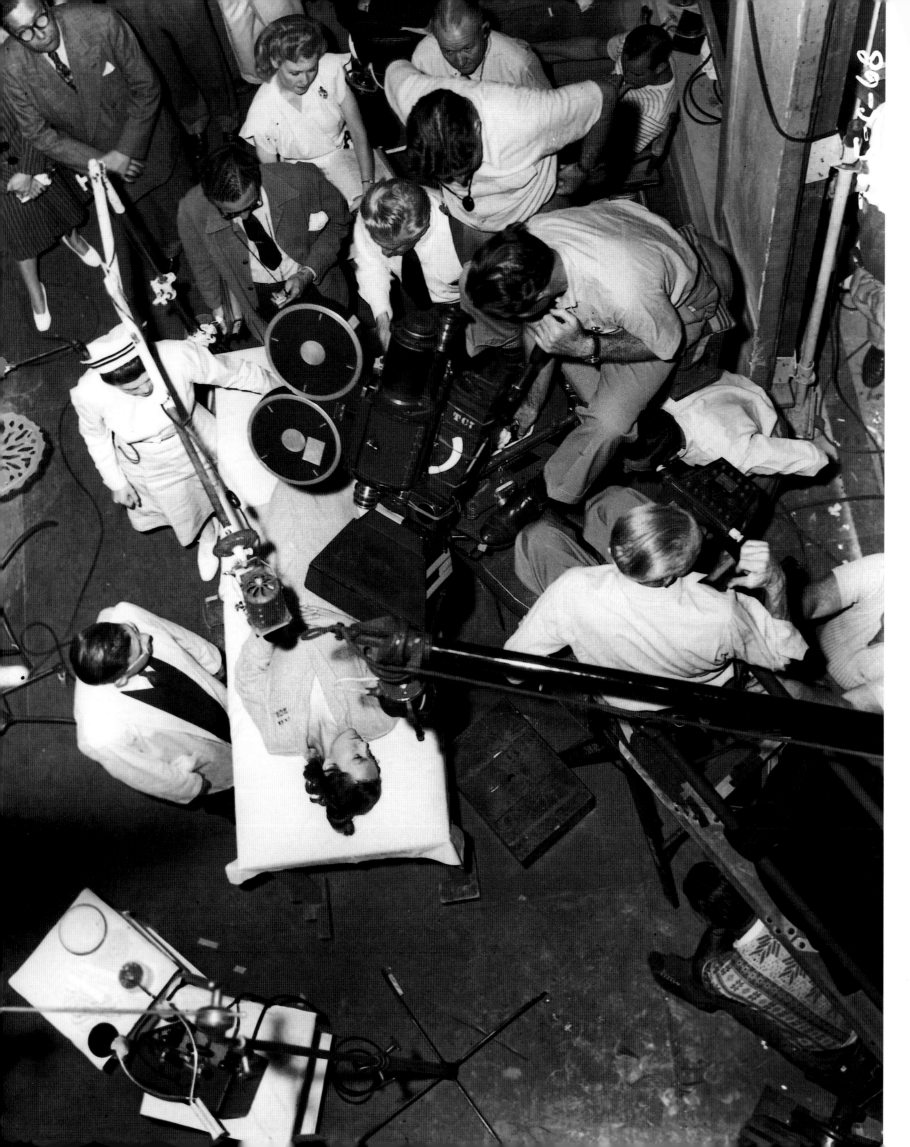

PREVIOUS SPREAD

THE SNOWS OF
KILIMANJARO, 1952
Ava Gardner

THE SNAKE PIT, 1948
Olivia de Havilland
Photographer: Jim Reid

LOVE IS A MANY-
SPLENDORED THING, 1955
Jennifer Jones

ANNE OF THE INDIES, 1951
Louis Jourdan and Debra Paget

TITANIC, 1997
Photographer: Charlie Arneson

MINORITY REPORT, 2002
Tom Cruise
Photographer: David James

Snow-making machine, 1949

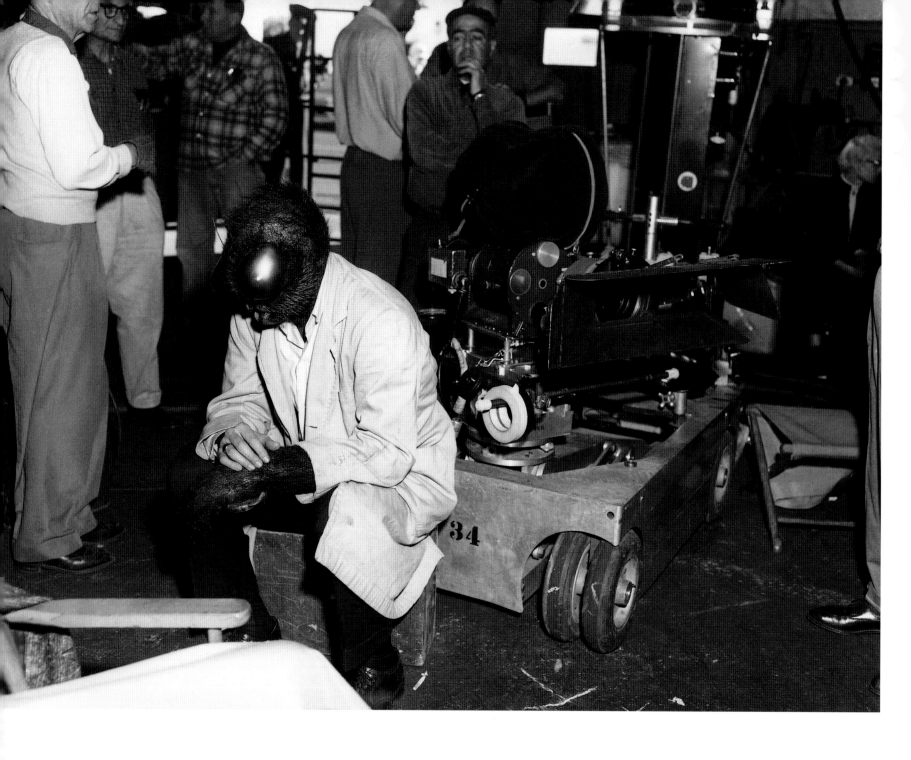

THE FLY, 1958
David Hedison

ROAD HOUSE, 1948
Celeste Holm

ROXIE HART, 1942
Ginger Rogers

ALL ABOUT EVE, 1950
Joseph Mankiewicz and Bette Davis

THE KING AND I, 1956
Michiko Iseri and Yuriko

THE THREE MUSKETEERS, 1939
Georges Renavent and Don Ameche

THE RAINS CAME, 1939
Myrna Loy

THREE BLIND MICE, 1938
Loretta Young

CAFE METROPOLE, 1937
Loretta Young

ON THE RIVIERA, 1951
Walter Lang and Gene Tierney

THE RAINS CAME, 1939
Tyrone Power and Myrna Loy

GEORGE WHITE'S SCANDALS, 1934
Rudy Vallee and Alice Faye

CUMMINGS A-400
SET #25

SWEET ROSIE O'GRADY, 1943   JITTERBUGS, 1943

THE LONGEST DAY, 1962

THE LONGEST DAY, 1962
Darryl Zanuck

GENTLEMEN PREFER BLONDES, 1953   NIGHT AND THE CITY, c. 1950
Jane Russell

VALLEY OF THE DOLLS, 1967
Sharon Tate

MOTHER, JUGGS & SPEED, 1976
Raquel Welch and Harvey Keitel
Photographer: Douglas Kirkland

IN LIKE FLINT, 1967
James Coburn and Thomas Hasson

THE HUNTERS, 1958
Robert Wagner

A GUIDE FOR THE
MARRIED MAN, 1967
Carl Reiner

LEAVE HER TO HEAVEN, 1945
Gene Tierney

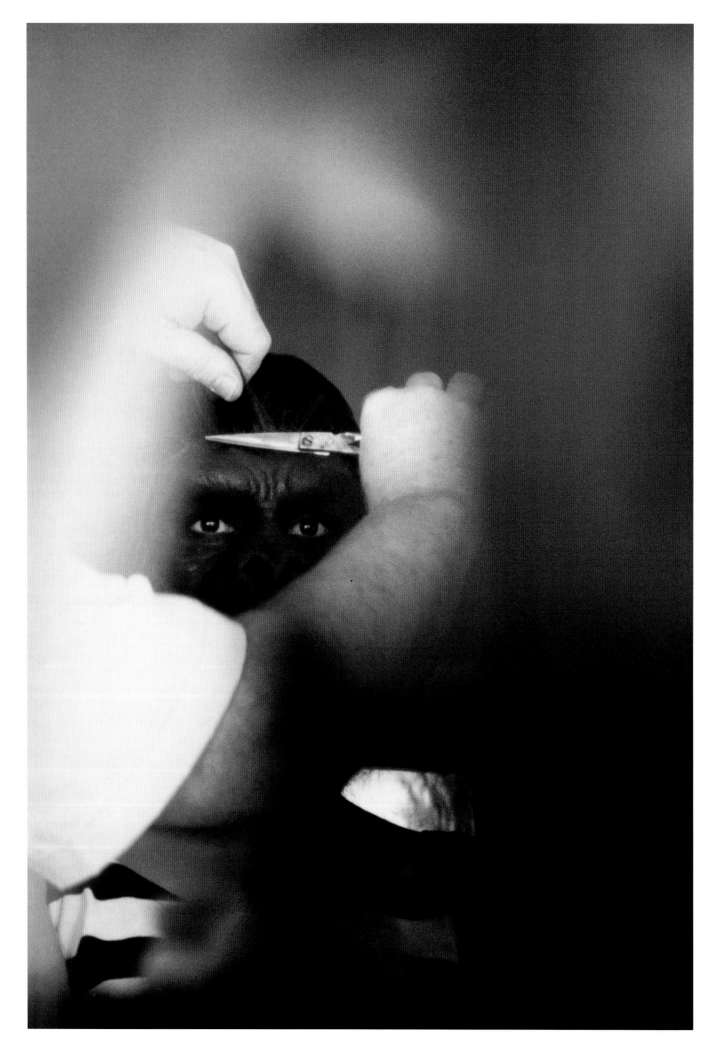

SAY ONE FOR ME, 1959   STAR!, 1968

STORMY WEATHER, 1943   THE GANG'S ALL HERE, 1943

SUSANNAH OF THE
MOUNTIES, 1939

The Commissary staff, 1936

JUST IMAGINE, 1930
Joyzelle Joyner
Photographer: Max Munn Autrey

THE ROCKY HORROR
PICTURE SHOW, 1975
Peter Hinwood
Photographer: John Jay

Susan Zanuck, Darrylin Zanuck, and
Shirley Temple at Richard Zanuck's
second birthday party, 1936

THE OTHER, 1972

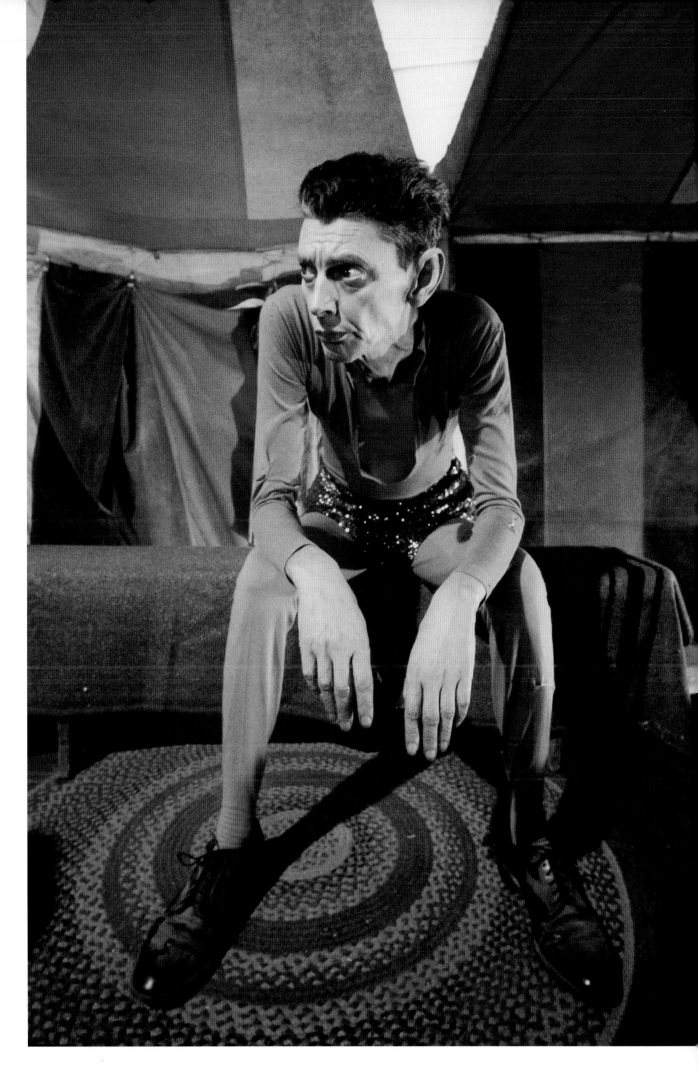

FOOTLIGHT SERENADE, 1942
Betty Grable (right)

THAT WONDERFUL URGE, 1948
Gene Tierney

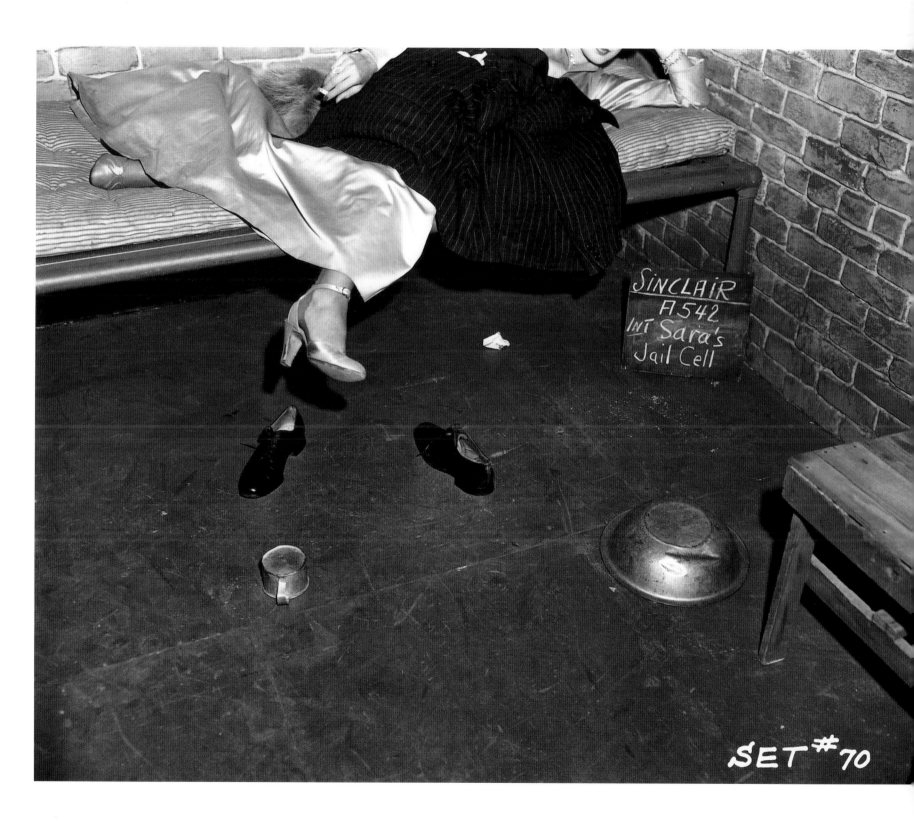

THREE CAME HOME, 1950
Claudette Colbert

THIS ABOVE ALL, 1942
Joan Fontaine

CLEOPATRA, 1963
Elizabeth Taylor

SATAN NEVER SLEEPS, 1962
France Nuyen

Jean Peters, c. 1950   Jeanne Crain, c. 1950

ZORBA THE GREEK, 1964
Lila Kedrova

RAWHIDE, 1951
Susan Hayward

APRIL LOVE, 1957
Shirley Jones

FANTASTIC VOYAGE, 1966
Raquel Welch

THE DAY THE FISH CAME OUT, 1967
Candice Bergen
Photographer: Constantine Manos

THE ANNIVERSARY, 1968
Bette Davis

KING OF BURLESQUE, 1935   BOTTOMS UP, 1934
Alice Faye

WILL SUCCESS SPOIL
ROCK HUNTER?, 1957
Jayne Mansfield

THE KREMLIN LETTER, 1970
George Sanders

THE LONGEST DAY, 1962
Sybil Burton

NO HIGHWAY IN THE SKY, 1951
Marlene Dietrich
Photographer: Cornel Lucas

802·S·93

MY GAL SAL, 1942
Rita Hayworth

HELLO, DOLLY!, 1969
Barbra Streisand

BERKELEY SQUARE, 1933
Heather Angel

THE THREE FACES OF EVE, 1957
Joanne Woodward

83x93

JOHN GOLDFARB,
PLEASE COME HOME, 1965
Joan Crawford and Shirley MacLaine

STAR!, 1968
Jenny Agutter

THOSE MAGNIFICENT MEN IN
THEIR FLYING MACHINES, 1965

CLEOPATRA, 1963

HUMAN CARGO, 1936
Rita Hayworth

CLEOPATRA, 1963
Richard and Sybil Burton

PREVIOUS SPREAD

THE BLACK CAMEL, 1931
Dorothy Revier

PATTON, 1970

TWO FLAGS WEST, 1950
Linda Darnell

THE KEYS OF THE KINGDOM, 1944   CLEOPATRA, 1963
Roddy McDowall and
Joseph Mankiewicz

146

HOW GREEN WAS MY VALLEY, 1941
John Ford

THE SOUND OF MUSIC, 1965
Robert Wise and Julie Andrews

HOTEL FOR WOMEN, 1939
Linda Darnell and Barnett Parker

CRACK IN THE MIRROR, 1960
Orson Welles

BELOVED INFIDEL, 1959
Henry King, Gregory Peck, and
Deborah Kerr

I CAN GET IT FOR YOU
WHOLESALE, 1951
Michael Gordon and Susan Hayward

THE LONG HOT SUMMER, 1958
Joanne Woodward

CONEY ISLAND, 1943
George Montgomery

LEAVE HER TO HEAVEN, 1945
Gene Tierney

THE DUCHESS AND
THE DIRTWATER FOX, 1976
Goldie Hawn

PLANET OF THE APES, 2001
Cary-Hiroyuki Tagawa
Photographer: Sam Emerson

THE BLACK ROSE, 1950
Orson Welles and Tyrone Power

MY BLUE HEAVEN, 1950
Betty Grable

ONE MILLION YEARS B.C., 1966
Raquel Welch

LIFEBOAT, 1944
John Hodiak, Alfred Hitchcock, and
Tallulah Bankhead

MAN TROUBLE, 1992
Beverley D'Angelo, Ellen Barkin, and
Jack Nicholson

DESK SET, 1957
Katharine Hepburn

TWO FOR THE ROAD, 1967
Audrey Hepburn and Stanley Donen

MOVE OVER, DARLING, 1963
Doris Day
Photographer: Jimmy Mitchell

CAN-CAN, 1960
Marc Wilder, Hedda Hopper, and
Juliet Prowse

CLEOPATRA, 1963
Elizabeth Taylor and Richard Burton

SAY ONE FOR ME, 1959
Alena Murray and Robert Wagner

UNTAMED, 1955
Rita Moreno

MOVE OVER, DARLING, 1963
Don Knotts
Photographer: Jimmy Mitchell

THE KEYS OF THE KINGDOM, 1944   THE FLY, 1958
David Hedison

CLEOPATRA, 1963

JESSE JAMES, 1939
Henry Fonda and Tyrone Power

CAVALCADE, 1933

HELLO, DOLLY!, 1969
Barbra Streisand

BUTCH CASSIDY AND　　　　　　Robert Wagner, 1956
THE SUNDANCE KID, 1969
Paul Newman and Joanne Woodward

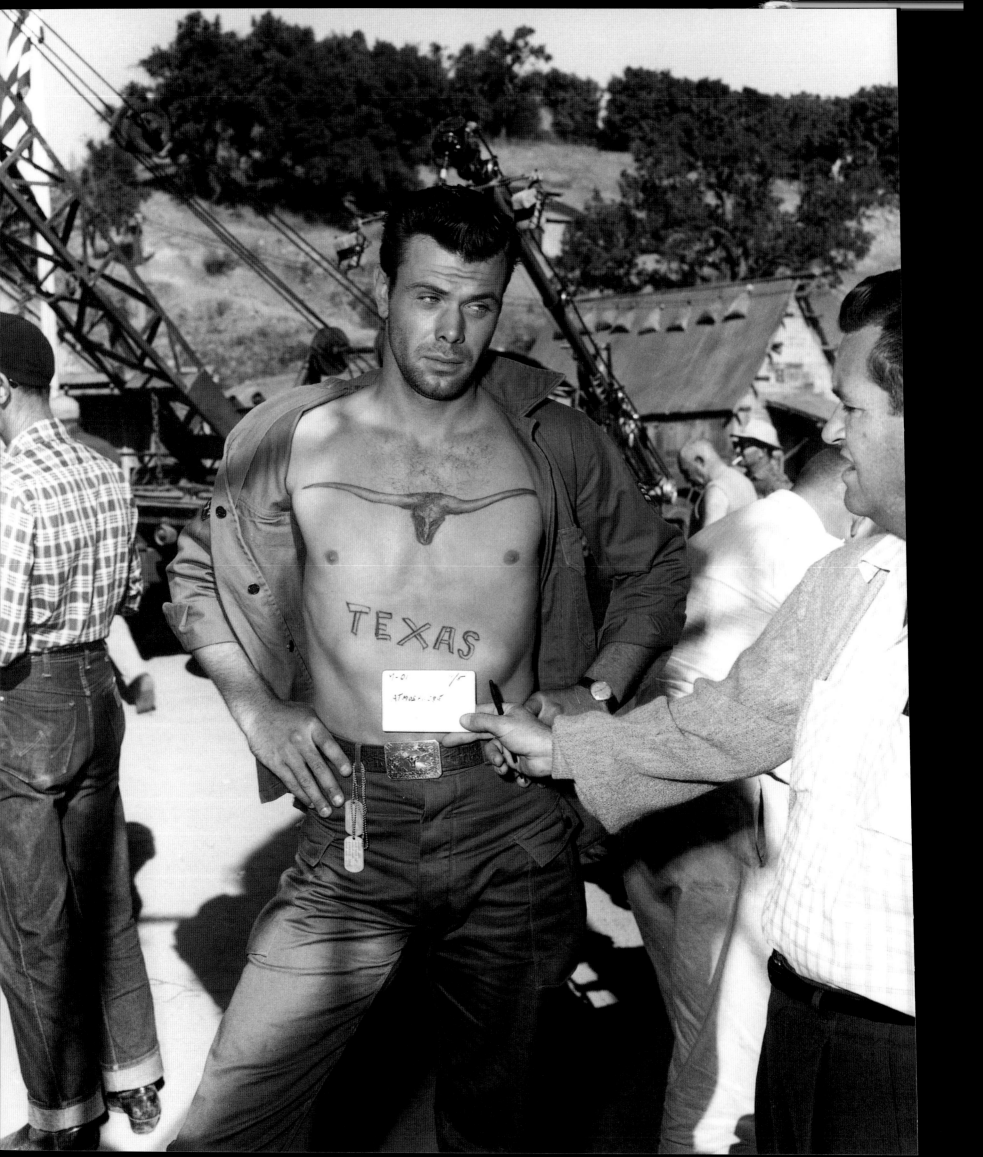

PREVIOUS SPREAD

WAKE ME WHEN IT'S OVER, 1960

HELLO, DOLLY!, 1969
Barbra Streisand

BENEATH THE 12-MILE REEF, 1953
Charles Wagenheim

THE SEVEN YEAR ITCH, 1955
Marilyn Monroe

DESIREE, 1954
Carolyn Jones

On the slate: DIRECTOR LEED'S SET NO. A 381 INT MURDOCK LIVING ROOM

SET #12

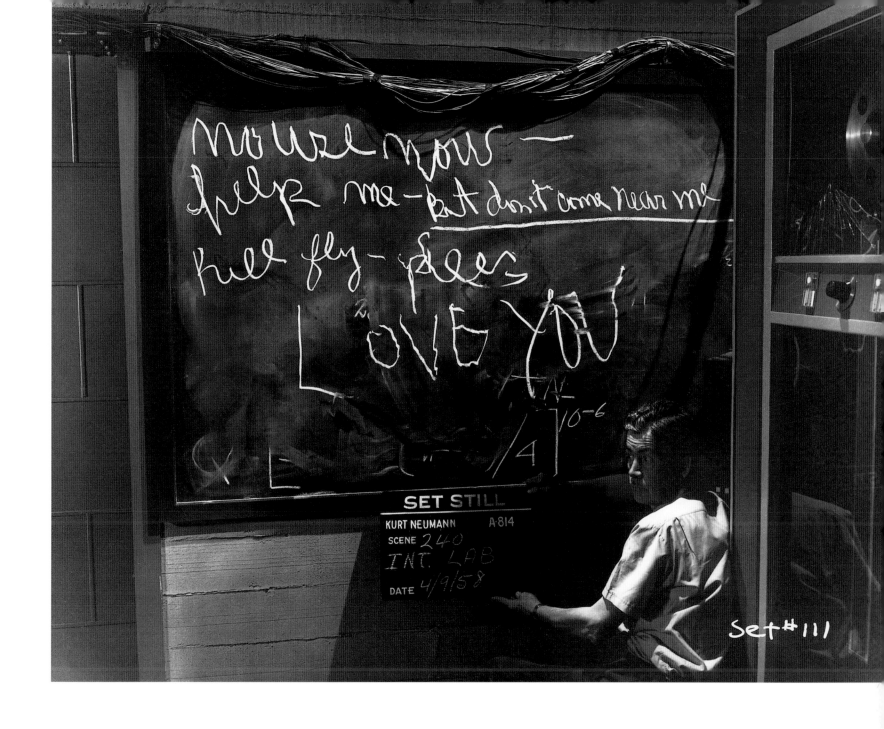

TIME TO KILL, 1943   THE FLY, 1958
Ethel Griffies and Heather Angel

GENTLEMEN PREFER
BLONDES, 1953
Marilyn Monroe

THE POSEIDON
ADVENTURE, 1972
Shelley Winters

957-5-57

THE WAYWARD BUS, 1957
Joan Collins and Jayne Mansfield

SAY ONE FOR ME, 1959

MYRA BRECKINRIDGE, 1970
Farrah Fawcett
Photographer: Bruce McBroom

JESSE JAMES, 1939
Tyrone Power and Henry Fonda
Photographer: Frank Powolny

THE YOUNG LIONS, 1958
Montgomery Clift

VON RYAN'S EXPRESS, 1965
Frank Sinatra
Photographer: Ted Allan

CRY OF THE CITY, 1948
Victor Mature

SET #85

HAL PHYFE

6

PREVIOUS SPREAD
HELLO, SISTER!, 1933
Erich von Stroheim
Photographer: Hal Phyfe

CALL HER SAVAGE, 1932
Clara Bow and Gilbert Roland

5 FINGERS, 1952
James Mason

Simone Simon, 1937
Photographer: George Hurrell

CALL HER SAVAGE, 1932
Clara Bow

Peter Lorre, c. 1938

ALL THAT JAZZ, 1979
Erzsebet Foldi
Photographer: Josh Weiner

THE TURNING POINT, 1977
Leslie Browne, Agnes DeMille, and
Mikhail Baryshnikov
Photographer: Louis Goldman

MY LUCKY STAR, 1938
Sonja Henie

HUMANITY, 1933
Boots Mallory

MILLER'S CROSSING, 1990
John Turturro
Photographer: Patty Perret

Joan Collins, 1957

RINGS ON HER FINGERS, 1942
Henry Fonda

HELLO, SISTER!, 1933
Boots Mallory

GEORGE WHITE'S SCANDALS, 1934

LA LEY DEL HAREM, 1931
Carmen Larrabeiti

NOSFERATU THE VAMPYRE, 1979
Klaus Kinski

THE BOSTON STRANGLER, 1968
Shelley Burton

ALIEN, 1979
Veronica Cartwright
Photographer: Robert Penn

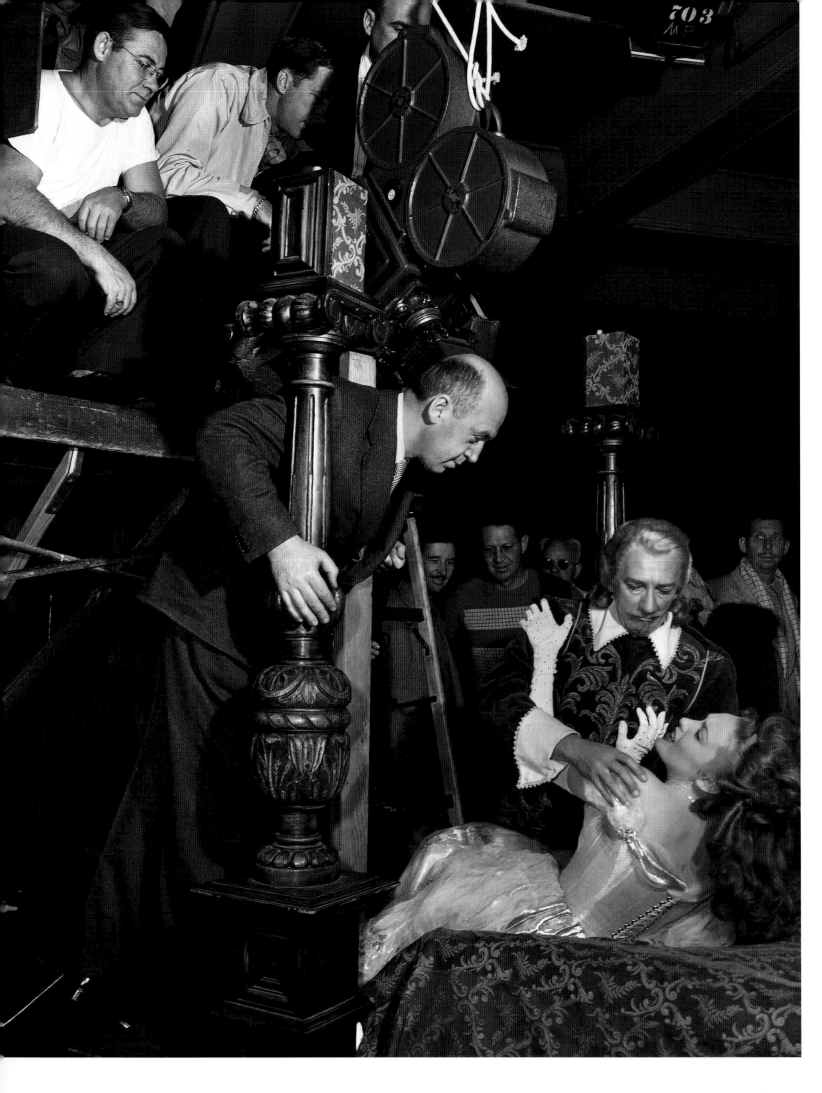

FOREVER AMBER, 1947
Otto Preminger, Richard Haydn, and
Linda Darnell

THE CRUCIBLE, 1996
Bruce Davison, Robert Breuler, and
Rob Campbell
Photographer: Barry Wetcher

FIXED BAYONETS, 1951
Samuel Fuller

MY BODYGUARD, 1980
Chris Makepeace and Matt Dillon

THE LONGEST DAY, 1962   THE AGONY AND THE ECSTASY, 1965
Charlton Heston

THE YOUNG LIONS, 1958
Maximilian Schell

CONQUEST OF THE PLANET
OF THE APES, 1972

TORA! TORA! TORA!, 1970   BUTCH CASSIDY AND
THE SUNDANCE KID, 1969
Robert Redford, Paul Newman, and
Jimmy Mitchell

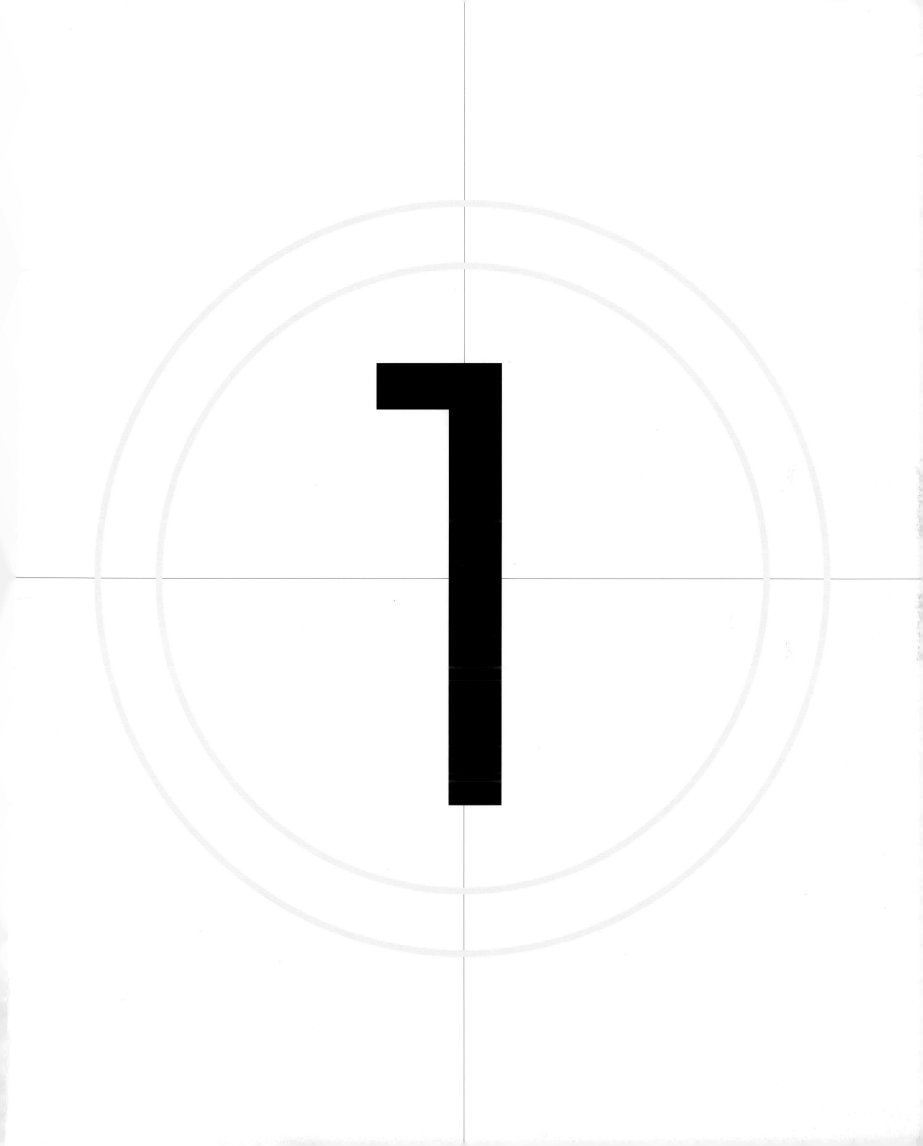

PREVIOUS SPREAD
CLEOPATRA, 1963

COCOON, 1985
Jessica Tandy and Hume Cronyn
Photographer: Zade Rosenthal

ALL THAT JAZZ, 1979
Leland Palmer
Photographer: Josh Weiner

STORMY WEATHER, 1943
Bill "Bojangles" Robinson and Fats Waller

DOWN ARGENTINE WAY, 1940
The Nicholas Brothers

ALL THAT JAZZ, 1979
Ann Reinking
Photographer: Josh Weiner

LISA, 1962
Stephen Boyd
Photographer: Joe Pearce

ALEXANDER'S RAGTIME
BAND, 1938

NEXT SPREAD
CHANDU THE MAGICIAN, 1932
June Lang
Photographer: Anthony Ugrin

START

FOR
PATRICK MILLER
(1947 – 2003)

FOX PUBLICIST AND GUARDIAN OF THE COLLECTION,
LONG BEFORE THERE WAS A PHOTO ARCHIVE

A SPECIAL THANKS TO THE PEOPLE AT
TWENTIETH CENTURY FOX WHO SUPPORTED THIS PROJECT

SCHAWN BELSTON
BONNIE BOGIN
J.R. DeLANG
JON DEL BARRIO
JANIE FREEDMAN
JIM GIANOPULOS
VIRGINIA KING
TOM ROTHMAN
JAMIE SAMSON
ERIC THOMPSON

WE ARE GRATEFUL TO THE FOLLOWING INDIVIDUALS
FOR THEIR ADVICE AND GUIDANCE

ALAN ADLER
STEVE NEWMAN
FRANK RODRIGUEZ
MELISSA TOTTEN

PHOTO LABS AND INDIVIDUALS RESPONSIBLE FOR IMAGE DUPLICATION

RUSSELL ADAMS, SCHULMAN PHOTO LAB
WILLY HALL, CRUSH CREATIVE
PRODUCERS & QUANTITY PHOTO INC.
DANIELE STRAUGHN AND TESS RULLODA, STUDIO PHOTO IMAGING, INC.
BILL VALENTINE, STILL PHOTO LAB, INC.
MARK VIEIRA, THE STARLIGHT STUDIO

FINALLY, A HEARTFELT THANKS TO ABRAMS AND PENTAGRAM, WHO,
WITH PATIENCE AND STRENGTH, SHOWED US HOW BOOKS ARE MADE

DEBORAH AARONSON, EDITOR
ERIC HIMMEL, EDITOR-IN-CHIEF, HARRY N. ABRAMS, INC.

ABBOTT MILLER, DESIGNER
JOHNSCHEN KUDOS, ASSISTANT DESIGNER, PENTAGRAM

FACING PAGE
THE MAN IN THE GRAY FLANNEL SUIT, 1956

The End
A
CinemaScope
Picture
Produced and Released by
Twentieth Century-Fox Film Corporation
THE
CHANTICLEER
GIFTS
GREETING CARDS